**DR F ATKINS
Resolutionary
Diet**

D0767443

DR FATKINS
Resolutionary
Diet

How to eat what you want and
pretend to lose weight

Dr I B Fatkins
Phd, MBA, FAT, MSN, TUB, CSE, MP3

PRION

First published 2004 by

Prion Books
an imprint of the Carlton Publishing Group
20 Mortimer Street
London W1T 3JW

ISBN 1-85375-534-6

Executive Editor: Roland Hall
Senior Art Editor: Darren Jordan
Editing: Gillian Holmes
Illustrations: Teri Gower
Typesetting: e-type, Liverpool

DISCLAIMER
The Fatkins Resolutionary Diet is NOT a real diet.
This is NOT a real diet book. This is a joke!
You should not rely on or adhere to any
of the recommendations given in this book.

Printed and bound in Great Britain

1 3 5 7 9 10 8 6 4 2

For people everywhere who like to eat real food

CONTENTS

WHO IS DR FATKINS?

By Professor Clint Mugfast

Professor Emeritus at the Ignatius Fatkins University, Milwaukee and author of *Fatkins – The New Diet Messiah, or Just Some Fat Bloke?*

Doctor Fatkins has over 50 years' experience in the food and dietary industries. Even in his teenage years stacking baked beans at the Clitheroe Co-op in Lancashire, England, his aptitude and understanding of the mechanics of food were recognized. His pyramids far outreached the piles of tinned peas and peaches erected by his colleagues. His rise in that industry was meteoric, and he was soon promoted from sauces and pickles to the cherished post at the bully beef counter.

The young Ignatius Fatkins had caught the food bug. But after three months in an isolation ward, and a diet of vinegar and potash, he was back, determined to make a name for himself in the emerging science of food. This, it has to be remembered, was the 1950s when the only constituents of the English diet were potatoes, sauces and pickles and bully beef, and the only diet book of the time was the much-used Betty Atkinson's *Potato, Pickle and Bully Beef Diet* published in 1873. Sauces were very much a 20th century phenomenon, but Betty's 1921 follow-up, *Sauce – A Soothing Foot Ointment,* merely showed that she had failed to keep pace with such a rapidly changing scene. She was to end her life gabbling incoherently to her grandson about the dangers of carbohydrates.

Fatkins worked hard at his studies and applied to read Complicated Science at a number of prestigious English universities. However, he suspected that England was already falling behind the New World in terms of dietary innovation and, on consideration of his rejection letters, decided to follow his chosen career in the United States of America. Sending off a cheque for $73, he received, return post, his degree in Food Science from the University of Poindexter, Illinois.

Intrigued to see his alma mater, Ignatius packed his bags and caught the first boat to New York. He would never look back – an unfortunate consequence of enjoying an afternoon stroll on deck when, as he followed the meandering path of a seagull, a sudden icy wind froze his neck. This medical condition has dogged him ever since.

America was a revelation. The words 'portion control' had no equivalent here and there were so many new foods to try – all fried, coated with sugar, wrapped in bread or smeared in fat. It all made such sense. The 350-lb Fatkins strode around like Slim Jim McThin as, with a self-satisfied smirk, he utilized many of the insults that had been thrown at him in the old country. Already the seeds of the now famous Fatkins Diet were taking shape – if he could feel this good about his body, why couldn't everybody?

Dr Fatkins had experimented with a number of diets, ever since he could no longer fit behind the wheel of his Hillman Imp. It had always been about 'giving up' – according to the latest fad diet of the time he had tried giving up breakfast, dairy products, and poached eggs, which just started him off on tying his shoe laces together, gnawing coal and even the craze of hopping before noon. Nothing had worked for him: he had lost confidence in the celebrity-endorsed Diana Dors diet when the once-svelte actress ballooned to 250 lbs in the time it took to film a shoddy B-Movie; and then the Berry Diet – based around a selection of berries and asparagus – left him with kidney malfunction after a mis-analysis of the dietary properties of deadly nightshade.

Meanwhile Dr Fatkins grew to love American fast-food culture, sharing his time between burger bars, fried chicken emporiums, donut diners and pizza houses. And, as his waistline increased, so did his curiosity: how come there were people here who could come through the door without having to turn sideways? People who didn't take up the whole of a double bench or who didn't work up a sweat carrying their tray back from the counter? After all, they were in here pouring unsaturated fats down them like they were banana milkshakes, stuffing down uncomplex carbohydrates and consuming enough calories to run a marathon. Why weren't they fat? Had they made some strange pact with God? Were they just lucky? Or had they stumbled across the holy grail of diets – the eat-what-you-like-and-never-get-fat diet?

From that moment on, Dr Fatkins made it his life's mission to discover what made these size-tenners special: how you too could eat 'the wrong things' and stay slim and how he could earn millions from gullible fools across the world. Letters arrived in droves...

...Fatkins has changed my life. Before my sister married him, I spent 15 hours a day on the sofa of our trailer watching sport on TV, drinking beer and eating crisps. My wife was a 250-lb slob with no figure and unable to walk without the static from her rubbing thighs causing a major fire hazard. Now, I am a Fatkins Executive, I have a mini-fridge by the sofa and can afford to buy brand-named crisps – my wife left me for a hot dog vendor in 2002, but she still comes by to wash up once a fortnight. I say give Fatkins a go… as the great man himself says, 'The only thing missing in donut, is u'. Spelling was never his strong point, but he can sure write a diet programme…

A BRIEF WORD FROM DR FATKINS

Let Me Introduce You to the New You

Hi! Dr Fatkins here. I expect you're thinking, 'Look at him: rich, handsome, self-assured, neatly manicured hands, beautiful spouse and an even better-looking car. I wish I could have just half of what he has.' Well, the absolute truth is it's pretty darn unlikely. However, thanks to my pioneering work in dietary science, you might be able to lead a more satisfied, fuller life and have a body to be proud of.

Welcome to Dr Fatkins' Resolutionary Plan. By buying this book you have taken the first step in making me one of the richest men in California and hopefully have done something for your own development as well. Read it carefully. I will say this before you start – it's not going to be easy. There are some big words and you'll probably have to skip the scientific stuff, but there are some pictures to look at if you get very bored.

Why, you ask, is it called the 'Resolutionary Plan'? You might not have asked but it is a rather clever conceit so I will explain. Firstly, I will ask you to make a 'resolution' to follow the plan meticulously. Secondly, you will need to be 'resolute' as you follow the plan through. See? They don't give away these Doctorates for nothing!

So are you ready for the new you? Ready to throw away the low-fat, low-calorie, low-carb tasteless produce that fills your shelves? Ready to abandon the sham of the afternoon aerobics class? Are you ready to tuck into some serious chocolate, crisps, pies and pastries? And are you prepared to throw away your wardrobe for some more comfortable clothes?

I'd like you to have a picture in your head of the new you... You, your wife/husband (because it's not just the girls who can benefit from Fatkins!) and your sweet-natured children are relaxing in your lovely garden outside your lovely house on a beautiful sunny day; you are looking great with a clear complexion, slim figure and great hair. Keep this picture in your head as you do Fatkins – it'll really help you keep going in those moments when the kids are crying, your partner has left you and you can't even get into supermarket own-brand clothes... and above all, remember, only a quitter gives up.

The good times are always just around the corner. Good luck...

Dr. Fatkins

Dr Ignatius B. Fatkins, 2003

CHAPTER ONE
WELCOME TO FATKINS

A Secret Shared!

Let me tell you something about *Dr Fatkins'
Resolutionary Plan* that none of the workers on the Dr
Fatkins' World Health Objective Programme will ever
tell you: *It doesn't work!*

Millions of women and men throughout the USA and
Europe – as well as a small group in the Inuit community
– who have exercized iron will and spent not inconsid-
erable sums on Dr Fatkins' Special Carbohydrate- and
Fat-Engorged products, will all testify that it doesn't
work. And that is the key. Once you admit that you are
not going to lose weight, that your figure is destined to
become more sun-dial than hour-glass, then you will
begin to find the programme much easier and may even
enjoy adhering to the draconian and, some say, sadistic
rules of 'doing Fatkins'.

For this reason, I never refer to it as a 'diet' (except when addressing groups of very deaf septuagenarians because it's an easy word to shout). The word 'diet' has so many implications: that you have to restrict yourself to a limited selection of foods; that it may be a temporary choice and not a lifetime's commitment; and that you may possibly be thinking you will somehow lose some weight. I prefer to call it a 'resolutionary' plan or programme with all its resonance of dictatorships and extreme punishments if you fail. But as this tends to scare people, I will often use the rather grammatically slovenly phrase, 'doing Fatkins', instead.

The Two Boasts

I have never been one to brag falsely (with the exception of the case detailed in 'The People versus Dr Fatkins: Fraud and Slander in Dr Fatkins' Lose-20 lbs-in-a-Week-or-Your-Money-Back Programme), but so confident am I in the 'Resolutionary Plan' that I shall make the following boasts, on my mother's grave*:

1   You will never be hungry whilst 'doing Fatkins'. If you follow the regular feeding points of the day, it

---

* Following the death of Dr Fatkins' mother just prior to publication, he has now put his dog's life on the line.

will provide enough calories, carbohydrates and fat for you to fancy a nice kip at virtually any time. However, I cannot stress strongly enough, Dr Fatkins' Number One Health Rule: if you feel a little peckish… p-p-p-pick up a Penguin. If a small chocolate biscuit does not satiate the hunger, it may be wise to make a sandwich or you will find that, usefully, many supermarkets now have spit-cooked chickens roasting throughout the day.

2   You will not experience any adverse health effects other than occasional biliousness, belching or flatulence (with the exception of those problems detailed in the chapter provisionally entitled: 'What's Your Problem?' at the end of this book). The body odour problem, claimed by some newspapers and scientific journals to be a natural consequence of doing Fatkins, is a scurrilous lie and anyway can be solved by using Dr Fatkins' Resolutionary Deodorant.

Case Study: The Mentor

Getting someone to help you with Fatkins may provide just the discipline you need. But be sure you find someone who will be strict and stop you missing out on those valuable calories and carbs.

Fatima was having trouble sticking to Fatkins. 'I kept

finding myself saying, "I'll have a diet cola – just this once", or "I'd really fancy a green salad with some low-fat mayonnaise." It was terrible, I thought I'd never be able to eat an Apple Danish again.' Then a chance meeting at Spud-U-Like changed her life. 'I saw Diane eating a potato with sour cream and looking like she was really enjoying it.' Diane had been on Fatkins for over a year and you could tell. She demolished that spud in minutes and was soon onto her second.'

Diane takes up the story, 'I saw her in the corner, looking a little ashamed of her potato without even a slither of butter and I remembered I used to feel the same. So I offered to take her under my wing. I've rigged together an electric shock punishment system for her; every time she misses a snack or declines a choco-late, I turn the shock up a little bit. She's very resilient though. Last night she took 2,000 volts before getting stuck into a Sara Lee Cheesecake.'

With her new mentor alongside her, Fatima is now getting along fine with Fatkins. 'Obviously, I twitch a lot now and sometimes shake so much I spill my banana milkshakes, but Diane is very understanding,' says the 34-year-old who has ballooned to 230 lbs. 'She just gets out the electrodes, smiles and says, "I think you want to lick that up, don't you?" For a weak-willed and, as Diane says, "pathetic specimen" like me, having a mentor is an essential part of Fatkins.'

Fatkins Key Point 5: Followers of Fatkins need to ensure they consume protein and vitamins.

Will it Work For Me?

In a word: Yes. In two words: Possibly Not. Have you got the will power, the physical strength and, most importantly, the money to do Fatkins? Have you got a wide selection of cake shops, fast food outlets and pubs within easy reach? Are you the kind of person who feels better for having someone else tell them what to eat? Whatever your answers to these questions, Dr Fatkins stresses that he does not do personal assessments.

Why Fatkins is Just Right for the Modern Dieter

The discovery of 'Brunch' in the 1970s was a watershed in my thinking. In one stroke it disproved that myth that there are only three mealtimes during the day. If brunch was acceptable, then surely so was a mid-afternoon snackette or a hearty cheese-on-toast supper. No more should we be confined to rigid meal times. Now, at last, everyone could stick to that old adage, 'Never eat between meals' because every snack could be a meal of its own.

For example, have you ever had that rumbling feeling in your stomach as it approaches midday? That's just nature's way of saying, 'Can I have fries with that please?' Remember telling yourself mid-way through an afternoon at the office, 'I'm not hungry, just a little bored'? Well, scientific research has proved that you probably were in need of some kind of chocolate bar, another 'meal' so to speak. And during mealtimes, why deny yourself? That second helping of roast potatoes at the Sunday lunch? You knew it wouldn't spoil anything really, that there would always be room for the rhubarb crumble even if you ate the whole damn roasting tin.

Remember, the body itself is the greatest guide, a finely tuned instrument that recognizes our needs to the nth degree. That is why doing Fatkins comes so naturally. It is really just a phrase book for the body. And, just as you wouldn't go to Spain without having the Spanish for 'Can you please direct me to an automotive representative?' handy; so you should be able to answer when your stomach says, 'I want something creamy, fruity with plenty of added sugar.'

CHAPTER TWO
THE HISTORY OF DIETING

Diets Don't Work

You can starve yourself, wire your mouth up, spend every morning in the gym, digest intestine-clearing worms (I don't believe this one has actually been tried yet but it sounds convincing) or eat huge quantities of meat until the fat drips from the corners of your mouth, but it's no good IT WON'T WORK. Dr Fatkins' programmes are the only ones that you'll want to continue with even after your optimum weight and shoe size have been obliterated from your mind. Other diets don't work because they involve eating stuff you wouldn't feed to your gerbil, or not eating stuff your stomach has come to think of as a great friend. Here's just a brief summary of some of the great diets of our age – and what was wrong with them.

THE 'BISTRO' DIET

The 1970s saw the diet up there with flares, big moustaches and Hi Karate aftershave. The chic 'Bistro Diet' was a hit with the young sophisticates in the new towns and was centred round an uninspired rotation of prawn cocktails, Black Forest gateaux, Babycham and a few slices of 'Nimble' (a special bread with all the dough taken out). Among those claiming to have lost pounds were Peter Wyngarde (TV's Jason King), Blue Peter dog Petra and the *Onedin Line*'s Martin O'Carthy (Midshipman O'Shaunnessy). The diet was to flounder after the controversial addition of foods such as 'Twiglets' to the advised programme – later blamed for the death of Petra and the unfortunate bloating of O'Carthy during a particularly steamy scene with Kate O'Mara. The popularity of the diet would peter out completely with the introduction of Vesta chow mein and the craze for turning maxi dresses into two-man tents.

WOK'S MY WAISTLINE?

BBC's Hong Kong Detective Charles Yap came up with this gem in the early 1980s. Yap, born and bred in Macclesfield, had 'discovered' the art of stir-frying and was evangelistic in his attempts to get the great British public to take it up too. Although it was low-fat and bulked out with low-calorie bean sprouts, his diet was largely based around the assumption that 800 million skinny Chinese people couldn't be doing much wrong. Unfortunately, the diet's main result was a 300 per cent increase in house fires and a huge great saucepan blocking everyone's limited kitchen cupboard space.

THE CANADIAN MOUNTIES EXERCISE DIET

The Mounties may always get their man, but this diet was never going to do the same for millions of house-wives. Their exercise and food programme had been carefully developed for the Canadian Mountie, to adequately prepare him to scour the forests and snow-covered slopes of Ontario. Unfortunately these activities differed considerably from those of your average person living in, say, Reading of Hull. An hour a day, grunting and stretching in front of the video, only succeeded in giving them thighs big enough to sustain a 12-hour horse ride, the beginnings of a thick black moustache and a penchant for maple syrup pancakes.

THE GRAPEFRUIT DIET

This was just one of a range of 'fad' diets based around a single ingredient. A typical day's menu on the Grapefruit Diet would involve: Breakfast – grilled grapefruit on toasted grapefruit skin; Lunch – poached grapefruit with grapefruit croutons; Dinner – curried grapefruit. When the supermarkets doubled the price of grapefruit in the great grapefruit crisis of 1986, women quickly turned to other citrus fruits – a dietary disaster that soon led to the elasticated waistband boom of 1987.

THE BEAN CURD DIET

This sensational new product promised the earth: filling; packed with vitamins; guaranteed to lose you weight; match your ying up with your yang; and take you to a higher level of metaphysical existence. The only problem was, it tasted of nothing at all or even worse – a bathroom sponge, after you'd squirted it with Matey and cleaned the bath with it. What promised to spark a new generation of thin, long-haired, flowing-robed brothers and sisters soon became a cue for millions to say, 'Does anyone ever eat that stuff anymore?'

THE HIGH FIBRE DIET

This cunning weight-loss plan involved finding ever more fibrous foodstuffs to fill your diet. It started out with eating a little bran for breakfast and trying to consume more pulses, but in the rush for fast results, millions were soon living solely on baked beans on wholemeal bread, cardboard and small pieces of carpet. Many called it the F-Plan, as it produced such flatulence that you had to plan ahead to arrange a time to discreetly pass wind. Although some did succeed in losing weight on this programme, many struggled to consume the necessary calorles to flnd the energy to chew their high-fibre foods. After one too many resuscitations of women found lying facedown in beans, the government saw fit to make all manufacturers remove fibre from their products.

There were of course countless other diets that came and went with as much, or even less, success. Some finished almost as soon as they began like The Blue Diet (eating only blue foods); The Y-Front Plan (going around in large underpants so everyone could see how fat you really were – the idea being that you would be shamed into losing weight); The Sea Food Diet (only eating while at sea); and the Slimquik Liquid Diet (drinking milkshake-type drinks after each meal until you felt sick). Others had a more scientific basis: the low-fat diet, the low-polyunsaturated diet, the high-polyunsaturated diet, the low-fat, high-polyunsaturated, low-unhigh-polycholesterol diet... Unfortunately you needed a degree in Food Science to understand them. The truth is none of these diets ever really worked. People got bored, had insufficient will power, propped the table up with the book or even, at the peak of their hunger, ate the book. It really did seem all up for the diet industry. People resigned themselves to looking like the bastard love children of

Fatkins Key Point 6: Make sure you ascertain which choice offers the largest portion.

Vanessa Feltz and Ricky Tomlinson. That is, until a new phenomenon raised its head...

THE LOW-CARBOHYDRATE DIET

Out of the blue, the 21st century produced the most user-friendly diet ever (that is until the Fatkins Programme emerged). Dieters were now able to gorge themselves on as much meat and dairy products as they wanted. The obese, unfit, spotty and often dirty-fingernailed state of our children, it argued, was not, after all, down to them eating too many burgers made from the parts of cows that even cows didn't like to touch. It was the hamburger bun that was the real culprit. What we had all been told to believe for eons: fat and calories – bad; vegetables – good, was now pronounced as hokum.

Carbohydrate was now the villain of the piece – the bread, potatoes, pasta and rice that we had all grown up on. Indeed, around the world, not so long ago, they were the goods that kept everybody alive. It turns out, that our great great grandparents were lucky not to be finding the waistline of their smocks getting ever tighter. In a bold re-analysis of the Welsh Leek Famine, it is argued that the starving inhabitants of Ireland should have been grateful, having been spared the indignity of having to ask for a size 20 dress or having to sit down to do their shoelaces up.

The diet swept the nation – as the traditional meat and two veg became meat and two more pieces of meat. As more people took it up, the worst consequence seemed to be the halitosis-breath that wafted out of dieters' mouths. It was, all agreed, a small price to pay for a population who could climb on a bus without getting out of breath. High amongst the evil foods listed were potatoes, carrots, turnips, apples, bananas and oranges and, as the diet became ever more popular, greengrocers were targeted: their windows were graffitied with such insults as 'Murderer!' and 'Carbohydrate alert – don't shop here'. Forced to go underground, they would hang around schools, shocking parents as they, sometimes openly, dealt 'carbs' to young children. Surely this madness had to stop…

To Fatkins… and Beyond!

And that's where Fatkins comes in. For some time I had been working on my own theories and the low-carbohydrate diet seemed to back them up. It was just that they had not gone far enough. Sure, no one wants to give up meat and cheese, but what about cakes, pizzas, kebabs, biscuits? And what's the point of a burger without a bun? A korma without some rice to soak it up? A roast without a Yorkshire pudding? I knew that, if there was a diet that said it was OK to eat fat, then there must be one that included carbs, sugar and really, really deep-fried chicken...

This is Why You Can't Lose Weight

We've all been there: followed the book to the word; got the kitchen scales out and made sure we haven't made ourselves one grain too many; followed some weird stretching exercise that meant we couldn't walk for a week; or watched the family pigging out while we nibbled on the cardboard that somehow passes for crispbread in Scandinavia. And we never lost an ounce. And I bet, like me, you blamed yourself. I was a walking guilt-bag until I discovered the real reasons I never, ever lost weight.

Subconscious Cheating

Don't feel bad. It's not really cheating as there is, scientif-ically, nothing you can do about it. The stomach is stronger than the mind – and that's a proven fact as many poor souls have discovered. No matter how much will power you have, if your stomach really wants that chocolate bar it is going to have it. Although not yet traced, it is believed that the stomach has direct links to the arms and legs and can override any instructions given by the brain. Many dieters have described how against their will, they have found themselves by the bread bin or at the sweet counter; one of my clients even found herself on a plane heading for a gourmet weekend holiday in Paris before she realized what she was doing.

Diet Myths

We've all been irritated by those career dieters who can reel off the calorific value, carbohydrate content and percentage of saturated fat level in every single element of your meal. Don't you wish you could knock that smug smile off their perfectly proportioned size eight body? Well, now you can as Dr Fatkins reveals the myths behind these figures.

For a start, carrots... how many calories in a common carrot? Ten? Thirty? One hundred? Would you believe me if I said 976? It is true, one carrot has the same amount of calories as three packets of crisps (except smoky bacon which actually has a negative calorific effect). Mistakes made in the original calculation of dietary values have never been corrected and years of repetition have created the myth. Other frighteningly fattening foods include spring onions, celery, chicken breast (white only) and bottled water (some of which is also illegally calorie-enhanced). Conversely, some of the best foods for those on a calorie-controlled diet have been slandered, including choc ices, peanut butter (crunchy only) and pork pies if you eat the jelly. No wonder your weight has been yo-yoing for years – all that misinformation has gone straight to the waist.

Metabolic Rate

No one who has read the book thus far will be surprised to find that I am at odds with the current thinking on the body's energy needs. Received wisdom suggests that a woman needs 1,000 calories a day and a man 1,500. Poppycock. Would the body really be as simple as that? We know that we all wake up in different moods, so would not our bodies as well as our minds vary day by day and even hour by hour? Just as many exercise diets have us working out to speed up our metabolic rate, so the Fatkins diet relies on understanding the mood of our stomach and manipulating it. For instance, you can get it in a good early-morning mood with a generous knob of butter – makes sure it is butter though, your stomach can pass the butter/margarine test with its eyes closed – and keep it sweet throughout the day with a selection of cheeses, sweets and one or two bottles of Alco pops. You'll soon find your metabolic rate has shot up and is working through anything you care to consume with a passion.

Nice Food Hunger

Hunger is, of course, a much more complicated biological process than indicated in diet books. One might say a good breakfast fills you up for the day, another that a meal without potatoes can somehow be filling. But us scientists know that there are many different hungers pushing and pulling your stomach hither and thither – often at the same time. There is the 'deep belly' hunger when it's 5 pm and you haven't eaten since lunch and your stomach thinks your throat has been cut. There is also the 'short solution' hunger, typically felt around 11 and which can be assuaged by a chocolate biscuit or, in more severe cases, by a blueberry muffin. And finally, and most important to recognize when doing Fatkins, is the 'nice food' hunger. When this hits you know it immediately – it's not peckish or stomach rumbling, it's a sensation that tingles across your whole body. You do not just need food; you need something specific – a curry, a generous helping of bread and butter pudding or possibly a Brie and cranberry sand-wich. On the Fatkins programme you must learn to recognize this pang and ascertain as soon as possible what your stomach is craving. The quicker you are able to satiate the hunger, the sooner you will be able to realize your long-term aims.

Fatkins Key Point 8: Food used for medicinal purposes is exempt from any calorie or carbohydrate count.

Case Study: The Incentive

Sometimes we all need that special reason to undertake a programme like Fatkins. Try setting yourself a goal, a time limit or just a certain pile of food you want to work your way through.

Steve was everything Marie had ever wanted – tall, dark, handsome with his own built-in kitchen and a complete set of Moulineux accessories. And when he proposed, it made her the happiest woman ever. And then the bottom fell out of her world – he'd only marry her if she lost 50 lbs. 'I was distraught,' remembers Marie, 'but determined. I was going to lose that weight. I've always liked my food so Fatkins seemed perfect for me.'

Marie was like a disciple, buying all the Fatkins books, adhering rigidly to every rule and even sending me cards detailing her progress (please note: Dr Fatkins never replies to unsolicited correspondence). 'It was the best diet I'd ever been on. I was eating more and more and wasn't made to feel the slightest bit guilty. I had our wedding day marked in red on my calendar and, every time I felt I was weakening, I would look at it and a wave of hunger would come over me.'

Unlike so many tales involving men, this one actually has a happy ending. Marie continues, 'As the date got closer and closer, I could feel Steve taking more and more of an interest in my body. Finally, on the big day, I got my scales out of the attic and proudly stepped on. I had put on 48 lbs. Steve stormed off, but just seven and a half years later I met Wayne. He might not be as tall or, some would say, as handsome and he is ginger, but he's got a part-time job in Norfolk Fried Chicken. And we are so much in love.'

CHAPTER 3
QUESTIONNAIRE

What Can Fatkins Do For You?

1. What is the first thing you do when you get up in the morning?
   a) Let the cat in.
   b) Shower and dress.
   c) Get the milk in.
   d) Put the kettle on and make a bacon sandwich.

2. Breakfast is...
   a) Optional.
   b) A chance to eat well when your metabolism is high.
   c) A dilemma – toast or cereal?
   d) The best meal of the day.

3. What is your reaction if your clothes feel tight?
   a) Start on an immediate diet.
   b) Worry that you may be pregnant.

c) Think about buying new clothes.

d) Think 'hmmm... sexy'.

4. Have you ever been on a diet?

a) I live on a diet.

b) I once lost 40 lbs in four weeks – and put it back on in two.

c) I try now and then but never keep it going.

d) You calling me fat?

5. What kind of diet is the most likely to succeed?

a) A low-carbohydrate diet.

b) A low-calorie diet.

c) A high-carbohydrate diet.

d) A high-alcohol diet.

6. What has the most carbohydrates?

a) A pizza.

b) A packet of crisps.

c) A diet Pepsi.

d) Twenty Lambert & Butler.

7. What has the highest fat content?

a) A scoop of ice cream

b) A piece of Brie.

c) A dehydrated noodle meal.

d) John Prescott.

8. Which of the following would you order after dinner?

    a) An espresso.

    b) A skinny latte.

    c) A cappuccino.

    d) All of the above and a double brandy.

9. What of the following health risks are associated with low-carb diets?

    a) Kidney problems.

    b) Dizziness.

    c) Bad breath.

    d) Pizza withdrawal.

10. What do you consider a meal is incomplete without?

    a) A glass of water.

    b) Salad.

    c) Potatoes or rice.

    d) Chips and brown sauce.

11. Which of the following do you prefer?

    a) Low-calorie drinks.

    b) Low-fat spreads.

    c) Low-carbohydrate crisps.

    d) J-Lo.

12. You receive a deep-fat fryer for Christmas do you?
  a) Exchange it for an alarm clock?
  b) Use it sparingly?
  c) Try a deep-fried Mars bar just for fun?
  d) Experiment by putting all your meals in?

13. You are told you have a fat ratio of 23%. Do you...
  a) Think about cutting down on meat?
  b) Think, that's not bad for a woman of my age?
  c) Think, well that's about the same as Camembert?
  d) Think, I'll celebrate with a bacon sandwich?

14. Waking up in the middle of the night, you get up and...
  a) Answer the call of nature.
  b) Drink a glass of water.
  c) Pick at some of the dinner leftovers.
  d) Scour the fridge and cupboards for the ingredients for a doorstep sandwich.

15. You think donuts are...
  a) Indigestible.
  b) Incompatible with a healthy diet.
  c) A good treat for the children.
  d) Did someone say donuts?

Score 4 points for each 'A', 3 for a 'B', 3 for a 'C' and 1 for a 'D' and then tot up your points total to see if you could benefit from Dr Fatkins' Resolutionary Plan.

55–60 It's only a biscuit – just eat it!
Is the low-fat, low-calorie, exercise and healthy lifestyle really working for you? OK you probably look great, still get into your size ten dresses and could give Paula Radcliffe a run for her money, but how long can you keep it up? Analysis shows that at least one in four of you will be tucking into a chocolate bar by the end of the week. Another one will just turn up at the gym for a cigarette and smoothie in the cafe and yet another will be secretly pigging out on a stash of Hula Hoops they've hidden under the bed. So where does this leave you? Feeling sanctimonious, but as lonely as that crispbread and lettuce leaf on your plate. A delicate petal like you might find Fatkins a bit tough though, so try working yourself into it gradually – perhaps a peanut at a time...

45–55 Sticky Fingers, Guilty Conscience
You try hard to keep your diet going, but it's all too difficult isn't it? Do you find the fat comes off and then comes back the next week and brings some of its friends? Can you resist everything except temptation? The family needs feeding with decent food, friends bring round chocolate cakes and staying true to the diet

is impossible. Besides, there just isn't the time to follow all the rules properly. Where do you buy Japanese Bark Tea anyway? What you need is a flexible dietary programme that works for you. Try *Victoria Beckham's New Starvation Revolution*. Only kidding, please don't cry; I know it can all get a bit stressful and there is an answer: Fatkins can fit around your busy lifestyle allowing you to eat what, when and where you want.

25–45 Mutton Dressed as Lamb?

You think you're doing pretty well, don't you? But all that 'I can still get into my wedding dress... I was a size 12 then and I'm still...' doesn't convince anyone. You might say you can eat what you like, but we've seen you taking the skin off your chicken breast. And all that embarrassing writhing around on the floor you have to do to get those jeans on doesn't impress anyone. 'Fat Bottomed Girls' might make the rocking world go round, but in my neck of the woods they just get a lot of bitchy remarks. So smell the éclairs and wake up to the fact that you'll never be young and slim again. At your age it's OK to let yourself go, and Dr Fatkins has got the ideal destination and the guidebook.

15–25 Save Some For Us!

I'm sorry, but there is very little we can do for you... except admire your style and say, 'You go girl!' If there were an Olympics for eating, you'd be chasing gold. You have a well-balanced diet – fat and carbs in one hand, calories and cholesterol in the other – and can still make it to the fridge without breaking into a sweat. But it is still worth considering doing Fatkins. Imagine eating what you do now, but being admired for your tenacity in following the programme. Never again will you hear them whispering, 'Lard bucket' and 'When's milking time?' Next time it'll be, 'She's doing Fatkins... and it's beginning to show.' Come and join us, you'll be a double AA student, I'm sure...

CHAPTER FOUR
WHY FATKINS WORKS

The Resolution

Let's face it – we're all after something so I mean to start this programme as it's going to continue – as honestly as I can without admitting this whole idea is just a hollow sham concocted to part you from your hard-earned cash. I'll put down a resolution of just what my programme can do for you. In return, I need some commitment from you, too, a promise that you're not going to do the usual cheats. Like:

I'm feeling a bit under the weather, I'll start on Fatkins again tomorrow;

My husband has just called me a 'saggy-bellied sow with thighs of jelly blubber', I'd better lay off the crisps today;

It's my birthday, I'm allowed one day off a year;

Fatkins Key Point 7: If your companion eats more than you, the calories in your food don't count.

I need to feed the kids something healthy, it's easier to join them;

My husband has just left me for a size ten blonde, I'll prove to him I can be a size ten too;

I've just read that bit in the Bible about gluttony and everlasting fires. Kind of put me off a flame-grilled burger;

My doctor says that if I don't lose weight, I'll die next Thursday; and

I've just killed my husband and the blood has put me off my food.

So here's my resolution to you:

I, Dr Fatkins, resolve to help you live a fuller life, to enjoy your food without guilt and avoid hunger. By paying close attention to my rules, you will never want to return to your calorie-counting, carb-dodging, fat-trimming, cholesterol-curbing ways. Other diets tell you to throw away the scales, Dr Fatkins says throw away your mirrors as well, stop looking at your reflection in chrome chip shop counters, get rid of friends who say you look overweight, and don't call your mother if she's going to mention you not getting into that dress again. Remember Fatkins is a way of life… not a *weigh* of life.

And your resolution to me…

I, ……. [fill in your name here] being of sound mind, and a pound or two over optimum weight (although you wouldn't say it showed), do hereby resolve to follow the programme put forward by Dr Fatkins.

I resolve to ignore any comments regarding 'smells from both ends', kidney or other internal complaints or the supposed 'harmful' effects of Dr Fatkins suppositories.

I resolve that if I feel dizzy – I will find something sturdy to cling onto and continue the programme regardless.

I resolve never to go on *Tricia* or *Richard and Judy* or any such shows and moan about the doctor or bleat about how much weight I've put on since I've been doing Fatkins, Or how my husband has gone off with my sister and if she says she's under 250 lbs then she's a bigger liar than him.*

I also resolve to buy only Dr Fatkins' authorized products even if supermarket brand products are half the price (for a full list of authorized products, please send a cheque for $73 to Big List, PO Box 778235, Milwaukee).

* Menopausal women are exempt from taking this resolution.

Agreed? OK. Prepare yourself for the new you – a chirpier, brighter, fuller, rosy-cheeked (ignore any spots – we'll deal with that bit later) you...

The Science Behind Fatkins

The Fatkins programme isn't something I came up with in an idle moment. It is the culmination of 30 years' study of diets and their consequences. Over this time the programme has been honed and corrected and is a fitting tribute to many who have sacrificed themselves to the scientific process. Like Steve from Birmingham, whose consumption of burger meals for seventy-three consecutive days left him with severe gastroenteritis (but, every cloud has a silver lining, also a complete set of plastic ready-to-assemble Disney *Toy Story* characters). Or Doreen from Cambridge who risked alienation from workmates by recording the amount of grub brought to work in packed lunches and returned home the same evening.

Science is the silent witness behind any dietary programme and I have done my time in the white coat, proving Fatkins works. Test tubes half-full of carbohydrates, used syringes of insulin, a still warm Bunsen burner are proof for all who would question it. However, I know dear reader, that you are not reading this for incomprehensible equations, turgid details about amino-acids, scary stuff about hormones or depressing facts about metabolic rates – you just want reassurance that you're not going to explode after 14 days on the programme. For this reason I have issued the following statements that combine to form a comprehensive justi-fication of the Fatkins programme.

The following food elements are essential for human life: protein, carbohydrate, fat, calories and cholesterol.

No one food exists that can provide all of these essentials – although an apple-filled donut does come pretty close.

It is therefore necessary to eat a variety of foodstuffs in order to stay alive. It is the precise combination of foodstuffs that is the key to the ideal lifestyle. Don't worry too much about green vegetables, they make a negligible contribution and are not exactly 'tasty'.

The people I term 'lucky eaters' are able to eat any quantity of food and still maintain their bodyweight. You know the sort: they pretend they are down the gym three times a day and only have three leaves of lettuce for lunch.

This capacity is in fact within us all, but many people have a smaller 'weight equilibrium zone'.

They unfortunately need to work harder to find the right combination.

The unique aspect of Dr Fatkins' programme is that I believe the 'weight equilibrium zone' is found by eating more rather than less – it may be you need more fat in your diet or perhaps more carbohydrate – but by eating more of everything you'll find out quickly enough.

One day we will all be 'lucky eaters' until then I'm afraid you are just going to have to eat, eat, eat…

Is this you? Three Types Who Will Benefit from the Fatkins Approach

All well and good for your larger lady and those with a healthy appetite you might think, but it's not really necessary for me. Perhaps you are too busy to eat regularly and often; maybe you are secure and happy and have no desire for comfort foods; possibly you are happy with the size you are and really do have no desire to fit into that dress you bought five years ago but have never worn. Of course, you might also be the type who actually doesn't crave fat and sugar, in which case you are just too weird and there is very little that Dr Fatkins can do for you.

Below, I have identified three types of people who, for one reason or another, are not meeting their true appetite desires. If any of the following sound achingly familiar, then Fatkins might just be the answer.

The Busy Mother

Are you skipping breakfast because you are too busy preparing it for the children?

Do you sit down to watch *Tricia* and yearn for a biscuit that you forgot to buy?

Do you find your maternity clothes getting increasingly baggy?

Does your partner miss the curves and bumps of the pregnant you?

Do the children get to all the crisps and sweets before you?

Do you feel guilty stealing half the chips and dippers off their plates?

Do you sometime lack the energy to push the buggy back from the shops?

Do you find yourself nibbling on a Rusk mid-way through the afternoon?

The Career Woman

Do you curse the day they stopped providing biscuits at meetings?

Do you pretend to your senior executive colleagues that you have given up chocolate?

Do you make a big noise about skipping lunch and then hide trembling in the toilets when the sandwich cart comes round?

Do you go to the gym before work and dream about a full English breakfast for 30 minutes while on the exercise bike?

Do you only have a glass of white wine soda with lunch when you crave the whole bottle?

Deep down do you really, really hate fromage frais?

At business lunches do you squeal, 'just a starter will be fine' while desperately scanning the entire menu?

Does your fridge contain just a bag of salad, a lemon and a bottle of slimline tonic?

Is your evening meal invariably a sad heat-up, low-calorie Marks and Spencer's lasagne?

The Thin Woman

Do you split a large combination pizza with three friends?

Do you think milkshakes are just for kids?

Do you become so absorbed in work that you forget to have lunch?

Do you fight the mid-afternoon slump with a nap instead of a cinnamon Danish?

Do you make sure you have leftovers in order to make interesting soups?

Do you throw stale crisps out?

Do you think it's too much trouble to stop at a petrol station just to buy chocolate?

Do you get into such interesting conversations at

parties that you never quite work your way over to the food table?

Do you eat only when you are hungry?

The Point System

Like many diets, the Fatkins programme aims to simplify the consumption decision-making process (CDMP) by citing many recognized foods that arise in the diet in a numerical form corresponding to their fat, carbohydrate, protein values. By using our handy cholesterol ready reckoner (available from Fatkins inc for only $117), it is easy to assess how near you are to achieving your target points.

The CDMP

1. Work out your Reductive Value total by multi-plying your weight (in pounds) by your age (in months) and adding your house number and a figure bigger than six but smaller than 27. Your Reductive Value is individual to you and must be kept a secret. If it is lower than 43 it would be advisable to consult a doctor. A value higher than 4067 could win you a holiday on Dr Fatkins' private

island (ring 0800 EAT FOOD to see if you have won – calls charged at £6.50 a minute – please make sure the bill payer knows you are calling and see if he/she fancies a go too.)

2.   Each meal you consume should be divisible exactly into your Reductive Value – any leftover numbers or decimal points can be used for snacks during the rest of the 24-hour period, but will be void if carried over beyond this point.

3.   At the end of the day, multiply the number of meals and snacks you have consumed by your Reductive Value. The answer is your Divisory Value, add the number you first thought of to this and you should have 0. If you haven't, top yourself up with some late-night crackers and cheese or a cup of creamy hot chocolate.

4.   Those either undergoing The Fatkins Simplified Plan or just unable to do the maths should eat when they feel like it but make some pretence at writing numbers down at the end of the day.

Some Common Food Values

A full list of food values is available from Dr Ftkins Inc. Send a cheque for $73 to Food Value Big List, PO Box 778235, Milwaukee.

Fatkins Key Point 10: If you eat something and no-one sees you, it has no calories or carbohydrates.

Aardvark	43
Avocado	7
Beans (baked)	765
Beans (broad)	2
Carrot	1998
Digestive Biscuit (packet)	17.34
Egg	0
Ginger	12
Poussin	37.3333333
Quail	37.222222
Rarebit	666
Toast	1
Warminster Soufflé	43
Yam	(Not Available at time of press)

Fat and Sugar – the go-faster stripes on the Cortina of life

Dr Fatkins has pioneered the role fat and sugar play in diet. He has brought these unwanted lepers in from the cold and cried, 'Make fat your friend' and 'Snuggle up to your sugar cubes'. Recognizing that both play a, hitherto, unrecognized, essential role in turning drab uninteresting food into something scientists refer to as 'tasty', he has built his diet around these twin pillars of the palate.

Fat is a Flabbiness Issue

'FAT'. It's not a nice word is it? Everybody hates it and everything to do with it. Whether it's saturated fat, unsaturated fat, polyunsabtulated fat or polyunpolyunsabtulated fat, it always seems to be one of the bad guys. And, for dieticians through the years, it's been the Osama bin Laden of the food world. They've gone after it and hit it with their hi-tech weapons and, yet, it wouldn't disappear; it has oozed its way back. Well, I've got news for these guys – this Osama's our friend and it's time we welcomed him back.

Many years ago, I stumbled across an ancient French recipe that noted that by adding fat to the dreary, dry potato you could create a 'portion' (old French word for 46) of French fries. Inspired, he experimented with other foods and found that just by adding a few globules of fat to food he could make almost anything palatable – even common-or-garden vegetables.

Further Fatkins investigation revealed that the fat present in cakes and biscuits etc. is completely different to the fat around the waists of lard-buckets walking up and down the high streets of the land. For years, we've been misled by the similarity of the words. Without going into complicated scientific jargon, one is fat – delicious and finger licking, and the other is flab – squelchy, unseemly and frankly unattractive. As far as your diet is concerned this is a green light for grease and all those foodstuffs they've tried to stop you eating... Now if one day we could only find out what causes those rolls of what, for precision, we shall refer to as excess disgusting flab, we'll have cracked it!

A Spoonful of Sugar...

It may help the medicine go down, but it does a lot more than that! Ask my satisfied clients (for a full list please send a cheque for $73 to Dr Fatkins Big List, PO Box 778235, Milwaukee) who have discovered that digesting the correct amount of sugar can be the key to keeping that unappealing body mass in order.

Sounds great, doesn't it? Cream cakes, biscuits, chocolate until you drop. Sorry though, tubs, we're going to have to bring you back to planet Earth – or Fatkinsville to be precise. The body is a far more complicated machine than your tiny unscientific brain can get a grip on, so leave it to the experts, and listen.

Dr Fatkins' exhaustive scientific research has revealed that digested glucose ('sugar' in lay-speak) forms a chemical reaction in the stomach with foodstuffs that scientists call 'boring' foods (bread, pasta, crackers, Wheatos, Japanese seaweed fruit). This is sometimes referred to as 'a funny tummy' or 'something that disagrees with me', and is often mistaken for a bad thing, but is actually the perfectly natural breaking down of the flab particles. Too much sugar, however, will have the opposite effect – and earn you a one-way ticket to flabville. A tricky situation indeed, when you know that one more spoon of sugar in your tea, or one more chocolate from the box could be the difference between that size 16 black dress and a pair of lime green elasticated-waist, ezi-fit velour trousers. To help you, Dr Fatkins has produced a handy guide to hitting the right balance. I, being more scientific than you, call it the gluco-remasticationary level. My disciples refer to it as 'the heaving point'. Just after 'queasy' and just before 'can you fetch me a bucket'. Oh, and that's the time to stop.

Let's Go to Donutville...

So you may be busy or you may not be that hungry (oh yeah?) but you are keen to give Fatkins a chance. It can be a daunting prospect for those who have never really over-indulged themselves before. So let's take it one step at a time. You'll find there are opportunities for both snacking and pigging out, even in the most unlikely places...

The Kitchen

It seems an obvious place to begin, but in a world of fast food and home deliveries, it is easy to forget you have a food production centre right here in your own home. Even when you think the cupboard is bare, there are still a number of choices open to you. Be imaginative – remember almost anything, even green vegetables, can be deep-fried into a delicious – and about as nutritious as it's going to get – snack. Similarly, butter, spread thickly, can add valuable fat and cholesterol to even the dullest of crispbreads. Finally, make good use of the frying pan. It's often the quickest way of preparing food and the smooth coating of lard actually helps the stomach digest it very quickly and with little effect on your waistline.

On the Hoof

A busy day, socializing or work, is no reason to ignore your Fatkins resolutions. You will be surprised how much you can fit into a handbag if you plan ahead. Bars of chocolate will slip in handily alongside a book and boiled sweets (ideal for topping up the calorie levels) can fill the corners. Use soft rolls instead of sandwiches – you'll find, with a little effort, you can squeeze three or four in and still get the zipper fastened.

The High Street

The problem here is not where to go, but rather so many fast food outlets, so little time. I tend to favour the burger and fried chicken establishments where you can eat standing up. This way you can eat rapidly and the calories and fat will be distributed in double-quick time. But don't be scared to utilize the more traditional restaurants. Take a look at the size of some of the clientele at the BHS restaurant – those cream horns add up in the end…

The Mall

Malls are reasonably new to the UK, so it is worth glancing across the pond to see how our American Fatkins cousins have utilized the food hall. Here is a magnificent opportunity to sample the fattiest foods from around the world. In a matter of a few steps, a plateful of spare ribs can be added to a slice of pizza and some onion rings.

The Countryside

A problem area, but still manageable for the experienced Fatkins disciple. Village stores might look bare of anything but condiments and dull foodstuffs, but you should always be able to find a packaged Apple Pie even in the remotest of backwaters. Check out the till area, sometimes there will be locally made produce. If you are unsure of their carbohydrate and calorie levels, try doubling your usual portion just in case. More promising is the Village Hall or Fête. Unnoticed, country people have been producing some of the most cholesterol-clogged cakes and pies for generations.

CHAPTER FIVE
'DOING FATKINS'

Before You Begin

Setting out on Fatkins is the start of a great adventure. You've probably already stopped throwing the pizza offers away as soon as they come through the letterbox. But hang on there for a moment, friend! As for any adventure, you need to make sure you are well equipped for the road ahead. Do you know the difference between deep pan and deep-crust? Can you remove a chocolate stain from your blouse? Are you ready to use your exercise bike as a clothes horse?

On Your Side

Now is the time to tell your friends and loved ones that you are going to do Fatkins. Those you see regularly might need time to get in extra supplies for your visit; husbands, wives and children will have to prepare

Fatkins Key Point 9: A box of quality chocolates can provide your total daily intake of calories in a handy portable container.

themselves to watch you struggle through a double portion at mealtimes and then, of course, there is the bad breath (which, remember, we never mention).

They can also provide valuable support. Anything from pointing out new 'eat-as much-as-you-like' buffets to helping you stick to Fatkins with comments like 'You're doing so well', 'Have my chips, I didn't want them anyway', or 'No, I'm sure it's not your breath'. Perhaps they might even like to experience Fatkins for themselves (although ensure they purchase their own copy of this book).

Kitchen Utensils

Now you are going to be eating in a totally different way, you'll need to reassess your kitchen. Your priorities have changed and there is no point having anything around that will tempt you back to your old ways.

You will no longer need the following items:

Kitchen scales – Dr Fatkins' recipes are designed for guesswork and then add an extra bit;

Salad spinner – ok, you hadn't used this wedding present anyway, but you definitely won't need it now;

Casserole dish – are you seriously going to cook anything that takes longer than half an hour?;

Steamer – still think you cook edible food without using oil? It doesn't work and never will.

Make sure you have the following items handy at all times:

Chip pan/fat fryer – full of oil and ready for action;

Wok – you can fit in a lot more than a conventional frying pan;

Potato peeler – what if that longing for chips comes when the chippy is closed?

Scissors – packaging on so many convenience foods can be a drag if you are in a hurry.

Packing for the Fatkins trip

You are going on the journey of your life and who knows what kind of shape you're going to end up. Obviously clothes are down to personal taste, but if you're going to go round telling people you are doing Fatkins, I don't want you embarrassing me.

- Take your measurements – even in a month of so you might not be able to believe what the old you looked like;
- Throw away anything without a bit of give around the waist;

- Shorts provide plenty of hefty thigh room – but be careful, you could scare the children;
- Invest in a tumble dryer – you won't want the neighbours seeing the size of your new underwear.

The Induction Phase

And away you go. You're now free to begin the most liberating programme of eating and drinking ever. But be careful! Overdo it in the first couple of weeks and you could be in trouble – heartburn, nausea and that Christmas evening feeling of 'I just can't eat a single thing more' could all put you off Fatkins before you even start.

Live to Eat not Eat to Live

Learn to enjoy your food. If you've never been a big eater then listen to a few people who have. As soon as you have finished breakfast, you should be planning your lunch and, similarly, at midday you should have your evening meal menu fixed in your mind. Snacks can be impromptu, but in the early weeks it may be worthwhile jotting down a few notes, in case you are caught unawares mid-afternoon.

Twelve Rules of Fatkins

In these early weeks it is vital that you stick rigidly to the programme. These 12 rules will help guide you. Later, perhaps, you can have a less strict approach, but deviate from these now and you've wasted your time, my hard work and that of the publisher, editor, printer and bookshops.

1. Your daily food intake should comprise something that walks, something that flies, something yellow and a packet of flavoured crisps.
2. You should not eat before 7 am. In fact you shouldn't even be up by then. Sleep is vital for your stomach to sort the food into food types and rummage through it for goodness.
3. Pork Scratchings, or if they are unavailable, dry roasted peanuts should be eaten whenever imbibing alcohol.
4. Fish should only be eaten with batter or in fingers with breadcrumbs.
5. Leave vegetables for vegetarians. They are generally unkempt and don't care what they look like anyway.
6. Never eat meat that has been left at the supermarket till by a previous customer who decided not to have it after all.

7. Do not eat the small biscuits that accompany coffee at restaurants. They are flimsy and an insult to serious diners.

8. Follow 'serving suggestions' on packet and tinned food religiously (yes, even the garnish).

9. If the contents of packet food (for example, cereal) have settled during transit, top up with another packet.

10. Never eat fruit that has been used to garnish meals or drinks – it is purely decorative

11. If you have not consumed your target points by 10 pm. Run. The chip shop could be closing.

12. Sushi. That's raw fish isn't it? Eughhhh!

It'll Knock Your Socks Off

Within a few days of starting Fatkins, you'll find you are feeling completely different. You may find yourself out of breath when running for the bus, perhaps your belt will strain a little at the usual notch. But you won't feel a pang of hunger or guilt. And take it from me... that's worth it.

CHAPTER SIX
KEEPING IT GOING

Case study: A Friend Indeed?

It takes some guts to do Fatkins. Sometimes sacrifices are called for that you thought you would never be able to manage. But inner strength is incredible – especially when there is a packet of crisps and a coke as a reward.

They were best friends – Angie, Mel, Emma and Jools. They bought the same records, went to the same exercise classes and did the same diets. That was until one coffee break at work when Jools mentioned *Dr Fatkins' Resolutionary Plan*. 'You are *so* not going to do that are you?' said the feisty Angie. 'Yeah, that sounds really great – not!' chimed in Mel. Emma just nodded at her Daily Mail. 'Another Fatkins Dieter loses leg,' screamed one headline, 'Soap Star Felt Queasy Doing Fatkins,' read another. While her pals sipped their diet decaf colas, Jools stared at her walnut whip and decided, I'm going to give it a go.

Some mates they were. As her interests changed from clothes and music and gym classes to food and eating in general, they dropped her like a stone. But Jools was determined to see it through and she soon made new friends. The woman in the bakery always gave her a nice smile and she knew two of the young guys in FattyBurger by name (well, they did have it on their badges).

'That was over nine months ago now,' reflects Jools, 'and there's not a day since I regret. Not when they were taken to Top of the Pops by Boyz Express, not when they bought identical bikinis for the Club 18–30 holiday and certainly not when that dishy new aerobics teacher started.' She's had a hard time, but now, when they are sweating it out in the gym, she sometimes watches as she licks her Choc Ice and thinks, 'Who needs friends when you've got Dr Fatkins…'

The Weekly Regime

The great advantage of doing Fatkins is that there is a far greater variety than with other diets. There's basically nothing you can't have, but it seems an awful waste of a decent hunger to fritter it away on something that is basically rabbit food. In this guide to a weekly regime, I have been faithful to the traditional breakfast-lunch-dinner daily structure, but if you find this constricting feel free to be more flexible. Perhaps you will be the one to discover a new mealtime, as discussed earlier the discovery of Brunch in the 1970s proved a major breakthrough.

A Word or Two on Beverages

Skinny South American. No, that's not the name of the latest fashionable coffee, but it is the main reason for the development of the cappuccino. After years of folk from the coffee-producing countries getting skinnier and skinnier, scientists decided something had to be done. After many different applications, the addition of frothy cream and a liberal sprinkling of chocolate flakes created the near perfect beverage, and with the addition of a biscuit (three, if they are the dull Rich Tea variety), you are provided with an instant boost to all your dietary needs.

However, it is still wise to cut down on your tea and coffee intake. The caffeine will do you some good, but with fluid, ounce for ounce, you are getting very little in the way of calories. As an alternative, try a mid-morning hot chocolate with added cream – a sugar and fat injection when your body is craving it most. Diet colas are a definite no-no – they contain chemical sweeteners, which scientists still can't prove are safe. Better stick to the original cola drinks – the dangers of which have been well documented. A glass of cola is equivalent to ten teaspoons of sugar so that will save you a lot of wrist work when sweetening your other drinks. After 5 pm you should really be sticking to alcohol. Although initially an appetite-suppressant, after a few glasses you'll find it helps bring on a marvellous case of 'the munchies' and provides a great stimulant for eating fatty fast foods. A glass or two of wine also helps the stomach relax after a hard day's work and it will thank you for it overnight when it has only a reasonable supper to work on.

Breakfast

Famously, diets have labelled breakfast, 'The most important meal of the day'. Now, I wouldn't want to undermine its significance, but in doing Fatkins it is vital not to consider any meal above others. Controversially, I sometimes feel it is worth deliberately skipping breakfast to create that mid-morning stomach-cramping hunger that can lead you to an emergency chocolate bar, muffin and packet of crisps. However, if you are going to indulge in early morning eating here are some guidelines:

Fatkins Key Point 4: Ignore diets with scientific explanations – they must have something to hide.

CEREALS

If chosen correctly, cereals can provide a valuable supply of fat, salt and sugar for the day ahead. Obviously a handy tip is to head for anything beginning 'choco' although so-called fruit-based cereals thankfully often lack any real fruit and really do the business as far as sugar is concerned. Breakfast muesli, on the other hand, is one of the most misleading foods to emerge from the myths of 50 years of diets. One bowl could destroy your Fatkins objectives, as its only effect is to clog up the intestinal workings and prevent you enjoying any food until well after lunch. There is very little worth eating in any muesli apart from the odd hazelnut, coconut flake and perhaps a raisin, but don't throw the boxes away yet – many a desperate, late-night search for sustenance has ended by carefully picking these very morsels out.

TOAST

When toast was invented in the late-15th century by Duke Ferdinand T'oast of Kettering, it was shunned by medieval dietrists as 'a foul abomination that clingeth to the mouth and is indigestible by the lung'. It was only when, almost a century later, a young peasant girl came up with the idea of spreading butter thickly across it that it really caught on. It was good enough for Elizabethans, Cromwellians,

Victorians, those fighting World Wars... but oh no...
our fancy 20th century diet-writers sought fit to
condemn it to history. Well, here's news... Fatkins
says, 'Toast is tops' – easy to make, plenty of butter
can melt its way in and there are a thousand different
spreadable options. Fast food for the home... without
anyone saying, 'Would you like a drink with that?'

THE GREAT BRITISH FRY-UP

With fat oozing from every inch of food on the plate,
carbohydrates packing your fried bread and hash
browns, and sugar bursting from the half gallon of
tomato sauce, you can guess what Dr Fatkins is
going to say can't you? Wrong! When you sit down
for an early morning fry-up, think again... You're
packing in everything that's good for you at a time
when your body is still half-asleep. Scientists have
proved that your stomach usually 'lies-in' for at least
two hours after you get up. Even then it wanders
round the body in a bit of a daze for a while
(depending what it's been up to the night before).
Eat that much goodness now and the stomach will
just give it a perfunctory going over. For this reason,
Fatkins has spent the last 20 years championing the
'all-day breakfast' – time permitting, a good fry-up
late morning will have enough in it to see you
through to a late lunch.

Mid-Morning Snack

Man's pre-historic ancestors enjoyed a much simpler, more natural understanding of their stomach than modern man. Unfettered by abstract concepts like 'hungry', 'tea time' or 'burger meal with free Disney gift', they were free to eat and drink when they chose. Interestingly, they would interrupt the morning mammoth hunt with a hot drink of roasted bark water and nibble on berries and nuts while discussing the finer points of the chase. So around 11 am, get back to the habit that came so naturally to our primitive forebears and indulge yourself a little. Not enough to ruin your lunch of course, but a small bite (perhaps a bagel) will keep your stomach ticking over and give some added fuel to your metabolism. You may also wish to make full use of the 11–11.20 choco-exemption period when any chocolate eaten will be automatically memory-wiped from your records. Generations of deliberate forgetfulness of morning chocolate purchases have led modern stomachs to discount calories consumed at this time.

Brunch

Americans have always had the lead on us Europeans when it comes to sensible eating – with the notable exception of grits. They pioneered fast food, TV dinners, peanut butter and jam sandwiches, chocolate-coated vegetables (still to really catch on) and brunch. The one definite rule for brunch is that it must be taken between 11.45 am and 12.15 pm so as not to interfere with other meals. Unfortunately, this can limit the amount you are able to eat. There are no other rules, but obviously the nearer you come to mixing breakfast and lunch – e.g. poached egg and Shreddies – the more points you earn.

Lunch

Now is the time to introduce the Fatkins' concept of 'defensive eating'. Imagine your day so far: you have enjoyed a hearty breakfast, perhaps picked a little through to your mid-morning snack and then topped up with an appetizing brunch. So far, so good. But looking ahead to the rest of the day, things get more difficult. There's a good couple of hours or more to go before the possibility of an afternoon tea and cake and a similar period before the evening meal. If you don't eat well at lunch, you could find all kinds of problems developing later – tiredness, perhaps dizzy spells, nausea and, worst of all, peckishness. For these reasons the guidelines of 'defensive eating' have been developed. They are there to ensure you have the fat, cholesterol, carbohydrates and calories to get you safely through the rest of the day.

FAT

Your 2.30 pm meeting started fine, but by 2.45 your
eyes were beginning to droop and an aching tiredness
engulfed your body. You thought it was the appearance
of the overhead projector, but actually it is your body's
desperate plea for fat. Getting sufficient fat to your
system in just an hour can be a daunting thought, but
take your lunch break seriously and methodically and
you will make it. If in doubt, fall back on the 'C-food
diet': crisps, chips, cheese and chocolate in the right
combinations will clog up your arteries just fine for a
while. If there are a number of people at your work-
place attempting Fatkins, you might wish to ask the
work canteen to provide a special Fatkins option –
usually a deep fried dish from *Deep-Fried Delights –
Dr Fatkins' Recipes for a Fatter Future.*

CALORIES

Another scenario: during the drive back from the
supermarket you were alert and singing merrily along
to the latest R'n'B classic from smooth American singer
R Kelly. So how come, just half-an-hour later, you're
slumped in front of *Neighbours* with the shopping still
in the boot, cooking gently in the afternoon heat?
You've been scrimping on the calories again, haven't
you? That roasted vegetable and hummus sandwich
may have looked fine in the fancy supermarket pack-

aging – but its basically given you enough energy to skirt round the frozen food section and then wait 12 minutes for your number to come up at the deli counter. You're a busy person! Small, ready-made sandwiches like that are designed for those with practically nothing to do all day – like soap-dodgers, weathermen and people working in marketing.

CARBOHYDRATE

Carbo = energy, hydra = water, the 'te' is just a compound noun ending (don't worry about this, it's for Fatkins linguists only). Don't be fooled by recent diets that have painted carbohydrates as the devil's own work, they just create 'energy water' for your body; a bit like Lucozade or isotonic sports drinks and are as harmless as that – unless you create too many bubbles (see section on Fatkins side-effects: Biliousness). For 'defensive eating', you will need to create at least two pints of 'energy water' an hour. That might sound simple, but a small buttered focaccia roll and a Diet Pepsi is only going to do you for 40 minutes or so, and that's only if you cross your legs for an hour after lunch. It might sound difficult, but try to 'double your dough download', remember you are eating for two – the you that's sitting down reading *Hello!* magazine and the you that is bustling around making everybody's world a little easier to bear.

CHOLESTEROL

Cholesterol has been confusing food scientists for a long time. Some think it is a dietary no-no, some think it's an essential component, and almost all have trouble spelling it correctly. There are, in fact, two types of cholesterol – one is beneficial (known as 'Good Cholesterol' or 'GC') giving you that lip-licking feeling, and the other ('Bad Cholesterol' or 'BC') is acidic and is the agent that creaks the stomach tighter – commonly known as 'tummy grumbles'. Obviously we need to create both kinds to survive, but even more obviously we want to avoid grumblings during a work interview or during an important scene in *EastEnders*. Cholesterol is derived chiefly from dairy produce, potato skins, mayonnaise and Chicken Enchiladas, but can be usefully topped up by placing a small amount of powdered-soup (any flavour) on your tongue.

Afternoon Tea

Eastern philosophy has a lot to offer the West (and let's face it, when was the last time you saw an obese Oriental – apart from Sumo wrestlers) and I have tried to embed some of their wisdom into the Fatkins programme. The ancient Japanese sect of Vimto had a saying: 'As the sun dips into the great south ocean, so enters the digestive into the mug.' I have, of course, taken some liberties with the translation – McVities Digestives only reached Japan in the early 1980s and before that they had to make do with a very inferior wheatmeal biscuit similar to many supermarkets' own brand versions in the West. The point, of course, is that, depending on the success of your defensive eating, you will need to dip one, two or possibly most of a packet of biscuits into your afternoon tea just to get through to 5.30.

Dinner

It's all been quite hard work so far, hasn't it? You've spent the whole day bound to some pretty restrictive dietary rules… Well, relax, now is the time to enjoy yourself. Almost. This is, after all, a diet… I mean a dietary programme. The good news is you can have basically anything you like – from a piece of cheese on toast to a five-course blow-out. But remember the point of this programme – the bit you probably skipped because it was getting a little scientific – keep *all* your food elements equally high. If you've let the calories slip during the day – maybe that Caesar Salad looked too good to miss – or if your fat level is dangerously low – perhaps they only had low-fat crisps at the kiosk – now is the time to make amends. The following are just a few evening suggestions; you could always combine more than one of them…

A NIGHT IN

A quiet night in doesn't have to mean a disaster on the Fatkins front. There is now a wide-range of tasty bung-in-the-oven meals with the kind of high nutritional ratings we are looking for. Give yourself plenty of time and steer clear of salad – it is a trap for the unwary and can fill you up in no time. Get plenty of sweets and snacks in and don't forget you've got them; leave large notes to yourself around the house to remind you. There's nothing like going to bed to be met by a sign saying something like, 'Remember! Walnut and maple syrup ice cream in the freezer. Boy is it good!'

THE CINEMA AND THE THEATRE

Don't be afraid to go out and enjoy yourself whilst doing Fatkins. For instance, a visit to the modern cinema complex can provide a problem for many people on a diet programme. Fatkins, however, offers so many different opportunities from hot dogs to popcorn to pick'n'mix. Possibly there is still not enough for you. No worries. Now it has become socially acceptable to eat in the cinema, why not take a plateful in with you. The theatre, however, can still be snobby about such niceties. You can, of course, make full use of the pre-theatre dinner options in local restaurants – these are often served at low cost and at high speed and even if you do miss the first act, don't fret, theatre is usually extremely dull and you won't have missed much. Do, however, remember to order your drinks for the interval and leave your seat a few minutes before the break to make sure you are at the head of the ice cream tub queue.

AT THE RESTAURANT – TEN RULES

1. Ask the waiter if it is possible to have an extra main course instead of a starter.
2. At the salad bar, fill the plate with croutons and mayonnaise.
3. Eat any bread served before the waiter arrives – they should soon provide more.
4. Check the chef is using lard, double cream and butter, not low-fat spread.
5. Ask the waiter if you can finish food left at other tables.
6. Skip any soup course – it is filling without providing sufficient calories, fat or carbs.
7. Remember to always take the French fries option never the new potatoes.
8. Even if you are full, ask to see the cake trolley; you never know when you can make room.
9. If offered ice cream or cream with your dessert – ask for both.
10. Always ask for a doggy bag – if the restaurant has any food remaining at the end of the night.

Booze or Lose!

It's time to come clean now. For many of you there is little chance of reaching your optimum intake. Realistically, even if you are consuming three good meals a day and snacking regularly, you're probably going to be falling short on calories and carbohydrates. But all is not lost. For those struggling to keep up, there is always alcohol. Beer, wines or spirits are all friends of Fatkins...

In the past, alcohol has been described as 'empty calories' but this is hogwash. Beer, for instance, is rich in calories, but has protein and vitamins as well. Admittedly there is no fat but this is easily corrected with the addition of nuts, crisps or pretzels. You'll find a night in the pub can provide all you need to keep on the programme.

Scientists agree that it is essential to keep the body full of water. Alcohol is almost all water, and the part that isn't water is almost pure carbohydrates. The alcohol is, however, a diuretic, which causes the water to flush out almost immediately. On the plus side, this will mean a continual topping-up process is required, and it will also involve a consistent work-out regime including deep knee bends (getting out of the chair), some running and squats.

Here are ten tips to get your drinking days off to a flying start.

1. Throw away any stoppers or vacuum-corks – once you open that bottle of wine, you've got to drink it.

2. Explore the world of cocktails – this is the ideal chance to get some fat into an alcohol-based diet. Try some creamy concoctions that have names far too rude for a book that could fall into children's hands.

3. Find an off-licence that will deliver – beer and wine can be heavy in bulk, don't scrimp just because you can't carry!

4. Experiment in the kitchen – you'd be surprised what can taste better with a shot of tequila.

5. Fancy an early-morning tipple? No? Have you ever tried one?

6. Try reducing the soda in your spritzer or leave it out altogether – you'll find you can fit a lot more wine into the glass.

7. Drink pints at all times. And if you are a woman, remember, it has been scientifically proven that men prefer women who drink pints.

8. Coffee can become an important Fatkins ingredient – if you add brandy, whisky, Tia Maria, Cointreau – in fact, forget the coffee...

9. Those on the advanced Fatkins programme advocate the use of a trip to the park with a small bottle of meths or white spirits.

10. Use a night on the booze to generate a morning appetite for fry-ups, pies or bacon sandwiches.

CHAPTER SEVEN

FATKINS FOR ALL

Surviving the Real World

No one ever said it was going to be easy. There's a world out there that is plotting your downfall even as you empty those biscuit crumbs from the bottom of the packet straight into your mouth. Supermarkets are full of diet and low-fat products, gyms seem to spring up where once cake shops ruled supreme and the papers are full of the latest low-carb diet. It's pretty hard to walk down the street eating from a jumbo packet of crisps without a few glares. But if you're serious about Fatkins, I know you will take it.

You might fail. If you do it is important to keep things in perspective: you can always make up the carbohydrates or whatever tomorrow, or even spread them out over the week. Don't think that just because you chose salad rather than chips that you have blown the whole diet. Don't believe that because you didn't have time for

Fatkins Key Point 3: Too much information can be confusing.

dessert at lunch, you have to miss out again tomorrow, and don't think that just because you enjoyed that aerobic workout that there's any reason to put yourself through that nightmare again. And certainly don't deny yourself and start leaving your potatoes or even missing meals. It's just a short step to running a marathon. You might be a lily-livered, weak-willed, spineless coward with the self-motivation of a limpet, but Dr Fatkins still believes in you – just. Now get up and get yourself something decent to eat. If you are struggling... here are some tips that might help get you through:

Enlist help from older relations – they survive on modern pensions and know what it's like to go hungry, so they'll be keen to help you avoid such an unpleasant sensation.

Forget to take a towel to work, that way you won't be tempted to join your work colleagues in an exercise class.

Pretend it's your birthday so you have an excuse to take cakes into the office.

Get some treats in for the children... you are bound to eat them on the way home.

Reward yourself for having an extra large pudding by going without a biscuit in the afternoon.

If you have to have a salad, make sure you swamp it with mayonnaise and oil.

If friends are skipping a meal together – join in, but buy some snacks for when they have gone.

If attending a tee-total business lunch, have vodka – it looks like water and leaves no smell on the breath.

Keep a picture of Posh Spice on the fridge and write, 'Dear God, never let me be thin' over it…

When alone, push your finger into your stomach and ensure you cannot feel your ribs.

Case study: Don't Keep Mum!

Don't be selfish. Fatkins is not just for you, but for the whole family. You're never too young to start eating junk food with Fatkins' Junior Club. They might never thank you for it, but you'll give them a start they'll never forget.

Carrie was never really one to worry about her appearance. Until she had children, and then she just couldn't lose the weight she'd put on. By the time they were toddlers, not only had she not lost weight, but she felt she just couldn't keep up with them. 'I'd get up tired,' recalls Carrie, 'and by time the breakfast nightmare was over –

cereal thrown everywhere, milk spilt, banana crushed on the tablecloth – I was ready to go back to bed again.'

And then a friend recommended Carrie tried Fatkins. 'The difference was noticeable almost immediately. I had loads more energy and besides, I was usually too busy eating my own huge breakfast to care what they were up to.' Carrie found Fatkins fitted in beautifully with the school run: I could get home, have a couple of courses for lunch and, by the time I'd finished the second glass of wine, it was time to pick the little loves up again. There was, however, still one problem: the blighters just seemed to be getting more and more energetic. I wondered whether it was something in their diet and that's how I found out about Fatkins' Junior Club.

'I did away with their irritating little carrot and celery sticks – which I only ever pretended they ate anyway – and replaced them with pizza pieces and burger meals. It all seemed so right. Now, it's never a problem getting them to eat their dinner and, when they play, they are much slower and get puffed out much quicker. It's made my life so much easier. I know they were unhappy about sitting out of school sports day and having no friends, but they stopped crying when I told them how slim Dr Fatkins says they will become – eventually.'

Fatkins' Junior Club

The beautiful young Whitney Houston, unfortunately now a victim of time's ravages, once sang: 'Children are our future', and, it's very hard to argue with that. If you've got one, two or more of the little cherubs, you'll appreciate just how difficult it is to feed them for that future. They don't like the smell of this, the colour of that and the texture of the other. You try mashed vegetables, vegetables with butter and hiding vegetables behind the chips before dispensing with vegetables altogether and just giving them the chips. Congratulations! You are already half way towards the Fatkins' Junior Club programme.

Fatkins' Junior Club attempts to do what no other dietary programme has ever achieved: to get the children on the programme before they are able to repeat the mistakes their parents have made. Fatkins may seem right to adults, but to children it is absolutely second nature. Putting them on Fatkins will mean they miss out on none of those little moments that make childhood so special. Like your first trip to a drive-in burger joint, those three hours of berserk hyperactivity after your first taste of orange squash, or the whole lunchtime you spent staring disbelievingly at your school dinner.

Dr Fatkins had children of his own (as the court is

still sitting, I am currently unable to give any further details) and realizes that the adult programme will not be ideal for children. For this reason and for the many other benefits, it is imperative that you enroll your children in the Fatkins' Junior Club now. For just $93 a year, you get a complete junior programme plus a free 'Fatkins is Wicked' badge, a colour-in and fill-in Fatkins progress chart and a birthday card signed by Dr Fatkins (posted to arrive within 28 working days of the child's birthday).

Celebrity Fatkins

Film Stars, sporting heroes, pop singers – all of these have denied having anything to do with Fatkins in the national press. And yet, for many years now, many of them have been attending my celebrity clinic in Hollywood (there is also a smaller English franchise in Nuneaton). The controversy linked to the programme has meant that they put their weight-loss down to a low-carbohydrate diet, some mystic pseudo-religious nonsense or a wild abuse of cocaine... anything but Fatkins. So, although I am unable to name names, here are some profiles of celebs who – if they had the courage – would admit that Fatkins has got them where they are today.

MYSTERY CELEBRITY ONE

This 'smoking' (a clue there) hot supermodel, once associated with Hollywood's Johnny Depp, came to me having put on 40 lbs in nearly as many days. With a tyre manufacturer's calendar shoot coming up, she was desperate to get her figure back. A programme of pies, pizzas and peanuts saw her lose the weight in no time and although she now denies it, you can still occasionally see her after closing time at Big Pete's Pie Factory in Warrington on a Friday night.

MYSTERY CELEBRITY TWO

It's a 'crying' shame (are you still playing at home?) that this footballer didn't make better use of his talents. He also could have made better use of Fatkins. Trim and fit, he came to me after a successful World Cup in 1990 in order to lose a few pounds. After a month of Fatkins he had, as is expected, put on 30 or so pounds. The programme of beer, chocolate and potato snacks was definitely working. However, as the new season beckoned, he abandoned Fatkins for training and has never been the same since. A sober warning…

MYSTERY CELEBRITY THREE

When it comes to Fatkins, this rock and roller really took the biscuit… and the burgers and plenty of fried

peanut butter and jelly sandwiches. His manager put
him in my charge after he was discharged from the
army in the early 1960s and he took to the programme
like no one else. The initial weight increase period
lasted longer than usual – through the 1960s and
1970s – but soon he began losing weight. Feeling that
his fans would still yearn for the familiar jump-suit
bulging figure of old, he faked his death and now
works as Senior Cheeseburger Consultant at the
Ignatius Fatkins University, Milwaukee.

Of course it isn't about celebrity success, but the achieve-
ments of the ordinary men and women. However, if you
are still waiting… there are some braver celebrities who
have been willing to put their name to the Fatkins cause.

Chart success that may have eluded the larger singer
came the way of Jurgen Pultermeir after he lost 120 lbs
doing Fatkins. His single climbed to number one in the
charts in Luxembourg and the follow-up reached
number 38. On the nation's *Pop Icon* programme, he
had been described as having 'the voice of an angel and
the body of a very fat angel' and told that his chances of
pop success were nil and the only time he'd make it on
TV was in a deodorant advert. But Jurgen persevered,
building his programme around hot dogs with fried
onions. He now stands a faint chance of representing
his country in the Eurovision Song Contest.

We believe all our Fatkins followers deserve gold medals, but for one very special lady that really did happen. Julia Redwood was a 300-lb eccentric, whose response to the taunting children of her neighbourhood was to take pot shots at them with her air rifle from her basement bedsit. For a year and a half, she refused to leave the flat and followed the Fatkins programme purely by using fast food deliveries. She is now the 130-lb Olympic Ladies Small Bore champion. No longer a recluse, she lives happily with Australian long-distance pole-vaulter Craig Barnes.

Are you a celebrity who has lost weight doing Fatkins and is prepared to be lampooned in the national press? Or have you seen any celebrities you suspect of being on Fatkins (perhaps at your local curry house)? Then please write with details to Candy Mintzepper, Celebrity Stalker, Ignatius Fatkins University, Milwaukee.

Fatkins Key Point 2: Other diets often leave you wanting more.

CHAPTER EIGHT
WHAT'S YOUR PROBLEM?

Can You Have Your Cake and Eat It?

Since Fatkins achieved widespread popularity there has inevitably been a backlash. We have heard plenty of noise about the 'potential' side-effects of Fatkins, from the faint-hearted liberals, lily-livered socialists, health cranks, doctors, surgeons, British Medical Association, Royal College of Nurses, Royal College of Music, World Health Organization, EC Food and Health Committee, the government, the US Senate and even Madonna. Have we done something to upset them? Apart from giving them a few tips on how they might develop a better relationship between their mouths and their stomachs? Is it our fault they haven't read the whole book? Is it our fault they take it to extremes? Is it our fault that they are so gullible that they believe the thing actually works?

Apparently, according to the US State Supreme Court, all these are indeed the fault of Fatkins Inc. Therefore our lawyers have insisted that we add this section to the book on specific potential side-effects. Please note by *not* doing Fatkins it is by no means guaranteed that you will not get these ailments anyway and a lot of other pretty disgusting things as well, so although it's your decision, think about it seriously... after all why would God have given you two kidneys?

Hiccups

This is a side effect that can be caused in the over-consumption stages of Fatkins. Although quite pleasant initially, it can become an impediment to speech and to further eating. If your hiccupping continues for more than two days, it is safest to make an appointment with your GP.

Sweating

The Fatkins programme aims to build up a limited capacity to sweat in order to 'skim off' some of the body water. This should be equivalent to a small patch six centimetres in diameter under each armpit. If you find you are exceeding this amount, take the following precautions: remove the shirt, washing thoroughly under each arm, then apply a liberal dosage of Dr Fatkins' Deodorant (please note this is an industrial-level deodorant — shop-bought sprays will be ineffective against the kind of sweat produced when doing Fatkins).

Body Odour

And so what? Do you think skinny types don't smell too?

Bad Breath

A lot of adverse publicity has been generated against Fatkins in this area. Nothing has ever been proved, and besides, I've been called 'ol' sewage mouth' ever since I was at school. It is a natural process for the body to regurgitate unrequired wind and something in Fatkins may encourage the egg and garlic wind to permeate to the top. But it is really about personal taste. In France, for example, a burpful of old egg and garlic is seen as quite sophisticated.

Limping Leg

Certain variations of Fatkins have been proved (by so-called scientists employed by an English tabloid newspaper) to cause a limp in one leg. This is caused by a surfeit of dough (right leg) against potato (left leg). By altering the consumption of the relevant foodstuffs, any such limp can be easily remedied.

Headaches

Fatkins' scientists are unsure of the origin of these, but they could be related to listening to endless news stories on Fatkins on television and radio.

Bitten-down Fingernails

This is a natural result of the constant eating impulse generated by Fatkins. All we can ask is that our followers refrain from this, it really doesn't look good (particularly when you nibble the skin as well) and I'm sure you can find something tastier to eat.

Stomach Ulcers

Doing Fatkins is no picnic for the stomach – it has to work overtime and weekends! It stands to reason it will develop the odd running fault. If you start to suffer stomach palpitations, cramps, excruciating pain or more than the odd rumble, don't be pathetic – it's probably indigestion or, at worst a touch of gastroenteritis. Ignore them and carry on eating regardless. If it does turn out to be Stomach Ulcers, you'll find out soon enough with violent vomiting and prolonged unbearable agony. Just think of it as another way to lose weight.

Heart Disease

Heart disease is a major problem that affects the whole of the western world. Over 62% of males and 48% of women will eventually die of it. So why on earth are they picking on Fatkins? Haven't they got anything better to do?

Kidney Failure

RESPONSE REMOVED FOR LEGAL REASONS. PLEASE READ DISCLAIMER ON PAGE 4.

Death

For a small number of people, Fatkins can be fatal. It is not known who is vulnerable or why it only picks on certain people. For this reason I cannot recommend strongly enough Fatkins: Am I likely to die a slow and painful death? Available for $73 from Fatkins Death Book Offer, PO Box 778235, Milwaukee.

Fatkins Key Point 1: Always keep to a healthy, balanced diet.

The New You

Hopefully, you will soon be seeing the early results of doing Fatkins. Don't be disheartened by the extra weight you might have put on. Use any disappointment to redouble your efforts and go that extra mouthful. You will probably be growing too large for many of your old clothes so use this as the first phase in creating 'the new you'. In your new wardrobe, I suggest you stick to blacks and keep it baggy – there might be a little more growing yet, I'm afraid.

But you have got this far – don't give up now! Remember, every little extra bit helps. Is there an hour in your day when you haven't had something to eat? Could you fit another potato on the plate? Could you get someone else to collect the kids for you (*Neighbours* is on and you haven't spent enough time lying on the sofa)? Are you still thinking FCCA (Fat, Carbohydrates, Calories... Anything)? Or are you sinking back into old routines? Just a small salad for lunch? Perhaps a diet drink this time? We don't really need a side order of French fries do we?

You need to remind yourself that the new you is just as loved, just as warm and friendly and just as good a parent as the old you – just a couple of sizes bigger. If it helps, think of it as letting the bigger person inside you get out. Once they are out, hopefully they'll buzz off and leave you in peace forever. And if they don't – well, perhaps you'll grow to love them the way they are.

As I said at the beginning of this book, Fatkins isn't a diet. And, as you will have found out since, it isn't even a way of life, it's a life sentence of hard labour. But work hard, do your time, keep your nose clean and you might be out in 20 years or so, looking leaner, fitter and, of course, older.

NUTRITION – YOUR QUESTIONS ANSWERED

Recent press coverage has suggested that those following the Fatkins programme put themselves at risk of nutritional deficiency. My first reaction is to say, 'Well, something has to go.' But, on further thought, I decided to add this page to the book. Some of the foodstuffs dealt with are unpleasant and unappealing and will have no effect on the Fatkins programme. However, should you be by a national press journalist, please pretend they are included in your programme.

Fruit

Fruit by itself is usually bitter and sometimes sour. Perhaps worse, is the effort required to peel many fruits compared with the ease of opening a neatly constructed cake box. However, relief is at hand in the use of fruit in many more pleasant-tasting dishes. If you are looking to up your Vitamin C intake, a healthy portion of *Duck à l'Orange* is recommended – this can be supplemented by candied or glacéd slices of lemon or orange. Please note, however, that the much nicer Chocolate Oranges actually contain very little orange and even Fatkins levels of consumption will not alter that slightly green look to your skin. The Fatkins answer is to take your fruit in juice form. Of the many varieties available, I recommend those with added sugar, reduced fruit and supplemented vitamins.

On a non-dietary level, many fruits such as lemons, cherries and bananas are pleasant to the eye and are a welcome addition to the home. Please remember to throw them away before they attract small flies though, as these could find their way to your more valuable supplies.

Vegetables

With the notable exception of the potato, vegetables contain little to interest the serious Fatkins follower. Like fruit, but lacking their sweetness, they are largely unpleasant to the taste and are generally without any aesthetic appeal. As mentioned above, deep-frying has some effect in nullifying their taste, but my advice is to use vegetables as a strictly medicinal necessity. If your doctor insists, it is possible to include a minimum number of green vegetables to the diet – but limit the list to frozen peas and the gherkin slice supplied with hamburgers.

Vegetarians

I am often asked: 'I am a vegetarian. Is there a variation of the Fatkins Programme that I could follow?' After I have stopped laughing, I admit that I find it difficult to eat an animal that smiles, but manage to get by and so should they. Although, it might be better to leave them tutting smugly as they look at the menus outside restaurants, Dr Fatkins has developed a supplement that should help them recoup lost fat and cholesterol. A secret mix of glucose and vegetable fat, it has only a small amount of meat stock in it to make it taste almost bearable.

Illness

If you find yourself suffering from any illness as a result of nutritional deficiency, please visit your doctor as soon as possible. Do not, however, mention the Fatkins Programme to him/her (the medical profession have an incomprehensible antipathy to Fatkins), but continue to follow the Fatkins principles: bear in mind the adage: 'Feed a cold, feed a fever'.

APPENDIX II
YOUR LETTERS

Though a very busy man, I try to find time to read your letters, however poor the grammar. Your problems, opinions and feedback on Fatkins are important to us. If you would like your letter featured in our next book please send it along with $73 to Blah...blah...blah..., PO Box 778235, Milwaukee.

Dear Dr Fatkins,
My husband disapproves of me doing Fatkins and said he liked me just the way I was? Should I continue on the programme?

Answer. Certainly you should. Who is he to define the perfect figure for you? You are a woman with your own mind and he will soon learn to appreciate that quality.

Dear Dr Fatkins,
I have been doing Fatkins for a year now and have noticed a change in my complexion with more spots than a school disco. Is this normal?

Answer: Doing Fatkins means you are imbibing more oils and fats than normal. Spots are just nature's way of expelling excess oil from your body. You might not enjoy walking around looking like a pepperoni pizza, but the alternatives are not pleasant and involve a long tube and some lubricating gel.

Dear Dr Fatkins,
It's me again. Are you sure I shouldn't listen to my husband? He does work in civil engineering.

Answer: The issue here is simple: who do you respect more, a naturalized American with a multi-million dollar publishing deal? Or a road-builder?

Dear Dr Fatkins,
Since starting on Fatkins, I have had great success, already putting on over 20 lbs. However, I don't wish to buy new trousers, just to find I can't squeeze into them in a fortnight's time.

Answer: Welcome to the world of Eze-fit elasticated waistbands. They're good enough for Alzheimer patients and American tourists, so what's so special about you?
Dear Dr Fatkins,
Thank you for your advice. Unfortunately he has now

left me for his personal assistant. My life is ruined and I am considering suicide.

Answer: I am sorry you do not seem to have the necessary will-power to see the programme through. I have been told to pass your letter to Dr Jenkinson who is compiling a research thesis entitled 'Fatkins and Clinical Depression – an inevitable conclusion?'

Dear Dr Fatkins,
My daughter is ten years old and still doesn't know how to order a cheeseburger and large fries with a chocolate slurry. Should I be worried?

Answer: Our Fatkins' Junior Club specialist writes: 'Children learn these skills at their own pace. Some of our ten-year-olds are still working on opening a pizza carton, while others have graduated to selecting a particularly fine claret to go with a *bouef d'agneau.* As long as she can open the fridge on her own, I wouldn't worry.'

Dear Dr Fatkins,
Every week we have to go to the mother-in-law's for a Sunday roast. She thinks Fatkins is just a here today, gone tomorrow gimmick and continues to serve up the same meagre portions. How can I make sure I get adequate food without upsetting her?

Answer: Sometimes we need to be flexible in our approach to Fatkins, especially when we might hurt others' feelings. Try eating a sandwich in the car on the way to dinner, sneaking off to consume a concealed bar of chocolate in the toilet or, if these are still not enough, tell her to get with the programme or she won't see the grandchildren ever again.

Dear Dr Fatkins,
I'm an air stewardess who has been on the programme for 18 months. I have now been threatened with the sack as I can no longer make my way down the aisle. I have been working for the airline for 25 years, how can they do this to me?

Answer: Discrimination takes many forms and this is one of the most unpleasant. However, if you've been doing it for that long you're probably not too pleasing on the eye and might put others off their food. Why not get a more suitable job – at the supermarket check-out or doling out school dinners.

Dear Dr Fatkins,
I'd like to pass on a tip that might help others who are doing Fatkins. I found it difficult to consume my daily calorie and fat quota, but now I set my alarm and awake at 3 am every morning. I find I can usually put

down a vital few pieces of toast and a creamy coffee.

Answer. I never cease to be amazed at the ingenuity, determination and sad lives of Fatkins devotees. It makes me weep – honestly.

Dear Dr Fatkins,
My husband and I have been doing Fatkins together. Last week a friend saw him in Muffins-R-Us with an old flame – he was eating a low-fat blueberry muffin. Should I confront him?

Answer. Don't jump to conclusions. There could be an innocent explanation. Possibly he had already eaten his double toffee muffin and was finishing her leftovers. Ask him if he still remembers his vows? Is he ready to turn his back on Fatkins and throw away all you've done together? Tempt him back to the programme – perhaps prepare something tasty and laden with cream for him when he returns from work.

APPENDIX III
THE FATKINS DIRECTORY

Since the publicity and success surrounding Fatkins a number of similar unofficial books have been found on the shelves. Doctor Fatkins bears no responsibility for the health and other implications of the following: *Dr Spatkins Eat Yourself Thin Diet*; *Dr Patkins Pancake and Maple Syrup Diet*; or *Dr Fatkiss's Big Belly Breakdown*. Please buy only authorized Fatkins products from the Fatkins University Shop or participating fast food outlets nationwide.

Fatkins Recipe Books

101 Things to do with Cream – saucy, spicy, kinky and you
   can cook with it as well!
Fryer's Tuck – deep-fried delicacies to help you do Fatkins
With a Little Help from my Fatkins – break that 10,000
   calorie-a-day ceiling
Fatkins for Vegetarians
Fatkins for Septuagenarians
Fatkins for Sagittarians

Previous Fatkins Diets

Junk Food... Junk Fat – slimming on a takeaway diet
Sofa... So Good – the couch potatoes guide to losing
   weight
Lard – the unacknowledged health food
The Donut, Do Nothing Diet
Lettuce – the enemy within

Other Fatkins Books

Fatkins By Name... The great man's autobiography
One Good Tern – 'If he writes as well on birds as he does
   on food, God help us all' *The Ornithologist*

Tern, Tern, Tern – 'Fatkins' tern obsession yields another classic' *Tern Monthly*

It's My Tern – 'Enough with the Terns, Fatkins' *Bookbuyers USA*

Associated Fatkins Products

The Fatkins Calendar

Fatkins fat-o-meter – are you getting enough?

Fatkins-o-matic – sugar in one end, fat in another – just press the button and it's an instant, heart-clogging delight

Fatkins elastictated waistband pants – Never again will you have to open a button or two halfway through a meal

Fatkins breath freshener – an essential for anyone doing Fatkins

Fatkins deodorant – Alpine fresh with a tantalizing hint of fried onion

My Diet Notes